Contents

Welcome to England!

Hello! My name's Benjamin Blog and this is Barko Polo, my **inquisitive** dog. (He's named after ancient ace explorer, **Marco Polo**.) We have just got back from our latest adventure – exploring England. We put this book together from some of the blog posts we wrote on the way.

A Benjamin Blog
and his Inquisitive Dog
Guide

England

Anita Ganeri

a Capstone company — publishers for children

Raintree is an imprint of Capstone Global Library Limited, a company incorporated in England and Wales having its registered office at 7 Pilgrim Street, London, EC4V 6LB – Registered company number: 6695582

www.raintree.co.uk
myorders@raintree.co.uk

Edited by Helen Cox Cannons and Tony Wacholtz
Designed by Steve Mead
Original illustrations © Capstone Global Library Limited 2015
Illustrated by Sernur ISIK
Picture research by Svetlana Zhurkin
Production by Helen McCreath
Originated by Capstone Global Library Limited
Printed and bound in China by CTPS

ISBN 978 1 406 29088 2
18 17 16 15 14
10 9 8 7 6 5 4 3 2 1

British Library Cataloguing in Publication Data
A full catalogue record for this book is available from the British Library.

Acknowledgements
We would like to thank the following for permission to reproduce photographs: Alamy: GL Archive, 7, Kevin Britland, 14, Michael Kemp, 15; Dreamstime: Anthony Brown, 17; Getty Images: WireImage/Matt Kent, 23; Shutterstock: Alison Henley, 22, Bryan Busovicki, 12, cristapper, 24, Emjay Smith, 11, Filip Fuxa, 27, Hugh McKean, 19, Ian Woolcock, 13, Jaime Pharr, 6, JeniFoto, 4, Joe Gough, 20, Jorge Felix Costa, 9, Kevin Eaves, 10, Kiev.Victor, cover, pdesign, 28, Peteri, 16, Phillip Minnis, 26, 29, Richard Semik, 25, Stephen Rees, 8, Steve Allen, 18, travellight, 21; XNR Productions, 5.

Every effort has been made to contact copyright holders of material reproduced in this book. Any omissions will be rectified in subsequent printings if notice is given to the publisher.

All the internet addresses (URLs) given in this book were valid at the time of going to press. However, due to the dynamic nature of the internet, some addresses may have changed, or sites may have changed or ceased to exist since publication. While the author and publisher regret any inconvenience this may cause readers, no responsibility for any such changes can be accepted by either the author or the publisher.

Some words are shown in bold, **like this**. You can find out what they mean by looking in the glossary.

River Tweed

SCOTLAND

Cheviot Hills

North Sea

Cumbrian Mountains

Scafell Pike

Lake District

River Ouse

North Yorkshire Dales

Pennine Chain

Windermere

Irish Sea

Manchester

Peak District

River Trent

WALES

River Severn

River Wye

Birmingham

The Fens

River Great Ouse

N
W E
S

0   25   50 mi.
0   25   50 km

River Thames

Bristol

London

Salisbury Plain

White Cliffs of Dover

FRANCE

Brighton

Seven Sisters

Isle of Wight

Cornish Riviera

English Channel

Isles of Scilly

BARKO'S BLOG-TASTIC ENGLAND FACTS

England is a small country in western Europe. It is part of the United Kingdom. England has a long coastline with the Irish Sea on the west and North Sea on the east. On land, it is joined to Scotland in the north and Wales in the west.

Historic places

The first stop on our tour was the fort of Vindolanda on Hadrian's Wall. The wall was built by the Romans to guard the border with Scotland. The Romans invaded England in AD 43 and ruled for more than 350 years. The fort was home for many years to Roman soldiers and their families.

BARKO'S BLOG-TASTIC ENGLAND FACTS

This is King Henry VIII, who ruled England from 1509 to 1547. He is famous for having six wives. His **portrait** hangs in Hampton Court Palace, one of Henry's many homes.

Coasts, rivers, lakes and moors

Posted by: Ben Blog | 1 May at 1.38 p.m.

From Hadrian's Wall, we headed south-west to Cornwall. It's a **peninsula** – a bit of land that looks like a finger sticking out into the sea. The coast here is amazing, with beautiful beaches and high cliffs. It's a brilliant place for surfing, so I'm off to catch some waves.

BARKO'S BLOG-TASTIC ENGLAND FACTS

The longest river that starts and ends in England is the Thames. It flows for 346 kilometres (215 miles) from near Cirencester to the North Sea, passing through London on its way.

We're here in the Lake District in the north-west of England. It's famous for its lakes and rolling hills. We've already climbed the highest mountain in England – Scafell Pike (978 metres/ 3,209 feet). Now we're off for a boat trip on Windermere, England's longest lake.

BARKO'S BLOG-TASTIC ENGLAND FACTS

Exmoor is a huge stretch of moorland in south-west England. It's home to wild Exmoor ponies, red deer and a legendary black cat, called the Beast of Exmoor. Yikes!

City sights

Posted by: Ben Blog | 4 August at 10.01 a.m.

Our next stop was London, the capital city of England. It's famous for Big Ben, the Tower of London, the British Museum and lots more besides.
Here's a snap of Barko next to one of the soldiers standing guard outside Buckingham Palace, the home of Queen Elizabeth II.

BARKO'S BLOG-TASTIC ENGLAND FACTS

London is a huge place, but not all English cities are as big as this. Wells, in Somerset, is tiny – almost 700 times fewer people live there than in London – but it counts as a city because it has a **cathedral**.

Good morning!

Posted by: Ben Blog | 18 September at 9.11 a.m.

English is spoken in England and by hundreds of millions of people around the world. It is the main language of countries such as the United States and Australia. A few people in Cornwall speak Cornish, a very ancient language. In Cornish, "good morning" is *myttin da*.

Welcome to
CORNWALL
KERNOW
a'gas dynergh

BARKO'S BLOG-TASTIC ENGLAND FACTS
Many people from India, Pakistan, Bangladesh and the West Indies have come to live in England. They have brought their own languages, beliefs and traditions with them.

In England, children have to go to school from the ages of four or five to 16. Many children stay at school until they are 18. After school, some pupils go on to university. The university here in Oxford is one of the oldest universities in the world.

BARKO'S BLOG-TASTIC ENGLAND FACTS

Many English people live in **suburbs**, just outside towns and cities. Some live on large, modern housing **estates**, like this one. Some people live in villages in the countryside.

It's Bonfire Night and we're staying on in Oxford for a party. On 5 November 1605, Guy Fawkes and a group of plotters tried to blow up the Houses of Parliament. Today, people remember this by setting off fireworks and building bonfires with a model of Guy on top.

Many English people are Christians and belong to the Church of England. They worship in churches like this one. But people who have come to live in England have also brought their own religions, such as Islam and Sikhism.

Fish and chips

We spent the morning sightseeing, then stopped off for some fish and chips. They're very popular in England. Another traditional English meal is Sunday lunch. You have roast meat, served with roast potatoes, vegetables, gravy and sometimes **Yorkshire pudding**. Yummy.

BARKO'S BLOG-TASTIC ENGLAND FACTS

People who have settled in England have brought their own types of food with them. There are many Indian restaurants, serving delicious curries, such as chicken tikka masala (chicken in a spicy sauce).

Anyone for tennis?

Posted by: Ben Blog | 1 July at 2 p.m.

Back in London, we're watching a tennis match at Wimbledon. Wimbledon is one of the most famous tennis tournaments in the world. It lasts for two weeks in summer and players come from all over the world. Wow, what a shot!

BARKO'S BLOG-TASTIC ENGLAND FACTS

The Proms are **classical music** concerts that take place every summer at the Royal Albert Hall in London. There are special Proms for children and families, and an open-air Prom in Hyde Park.

From bank notes to tourists

Posted by: Ben Blog | 9 September at 8.21 p.m.

London is one of the biggest **financial** centres in the world. It is famous for the Bank of England and the London Stock Exchange. The Bank of England is the second oldest bank in the world. One of its jobs is to **issue** banknotes and to guard the country's gold stores.

BARKO'S BLOG-TASTIC ENGLAND FACTS

Millions of tourists visit England each year to see its historic sites, such as Stratford-upon-Avon. This is where William Shakespeare, the famous poet and **playwright**, was born.

And finally...

Posted by: Ben Blog | 30 October at 7.34 a.m.

For the last stop on our trip, we've come to Salisbury Plain in Wiltshire. We're here to see Stonehenge, the most famous **prehistoric** site in England. The rings of giant stones were probably put up between 2400 and 2200 BC and were used for religious ceremonies. Amazing!

I am here!

BARKO'S BLOG-TASTIC ENGLAND FACTS

The White Cliffs of Dover in southern England are white because they are made of chalk. From the top, you can get a good view of France, but mind you don't go too close to the edge!

England fact file

Area: 130,279 square kilometres
(50,301 square miles)

Population: 53,012,456 (2013)

Capital city: London

Other main cities: Manchester, Birmingham,
Liverpool

Language: English

Main religion: Christianity

Highest mountain: Scafell Pike
(978 metres/3,209 feet)

Longest river: Thames (346 kilometres/215 miles)

Currency: Pound sterling

England quiz

Find out how much you know about England with our quick quiz.

1. Who built Hadrian's Wall?
a) The Anglo-Saxons
b) The Romans
c) King Henry VIII

2. Which is England's largest lake?
a) Windermere
b) Loch Ness
c) Grasmere

3. Who lives in Buckingham Palace?
a) William Shakespeare
b) Queen Elizabeth II
c) The Prime Minister

4. What sport is played at Wimbledon?
a) cricket
b) football
c) tennis

5. What is this?

Answers
1. b
2. a
3. b
4. c
5. Stonehenge

29

Glossary

cathedral large and important church

classical music serious music written by composers and often played by an orchestra

estate large collection of modern houses

financial to do with finances or money

inquisitive interested in learning about the world

issue send or give out something

Marco Polo explorer who lived from about 1254 to 1324. He travelled from Italy to China.

peninsula narrow strip of land sticking out into a body of water

playwright person who writes plays

portrait painting of a person

prehistoric from a time in the past before things were written down

suburb place where people live on the outskirts of a town or city

Yorkshire pudding English dish made from eggs, flour and milk

Find out more

Books

England (Countries Around the World), Claire Throp (Raintree, 2012)

United Kingdom (Countries in Our World), Michael Burgan (Franklin Watts, 2013)

United Kingdom (Discover Countries), Tim Atkinson (Wayland, 2013)

Websites

kids.nationalgeographic.co.uk/kids/places/find
National Geographic's website has lots of information, photos and maps of countries around the world.

www.timeforkids.com/destination/england
This website gives facts about England and includes a history timeline and sightseeing guide.

www.worldatlas.com
Packed with information about different countries, this website has flags, time zones, facts and figures, maps and timelines.

Index